EVOLVE

WORKBOOK

Samuela Eckstut

4A

T0268617

CAMBRIDGE
UNIVERSITY PRESS

CAMBRIDGE
UNIVERSITY PRESS

University Printing House, Cambridge CB2 8BS, United Kingdom

One Liberty Plaza, 20th Floor, New York, NY 10006, USA

477 Williamstown Road, Port Melbourne, VIC 3207, Australia

314–321, 3rd Floor, Plot 3, Splendor Forum, Jasola District Centre, New Delhi – 110025, India

103 Penang Road, #05-06/07, Visioncrest Commercial, Singapore 238467

Cambridge University Press is part of the University of Cambridge.

It furthers the University's mission by disseminating knowledge in the pursuit of education, learning and research at the highest international levels of excellence.

www.cambridge.org
Information on this title: www.cambridge.org/9781108408745

© Cambridge University Press 2019

This publication is in copyright. Subject to statutory exception and to the provisions of relevant collective licensing agreements, no reproduction of any part may take place without the written permission of Cambridge University Press.

First published 2019

20 19 18 17 16 15 14 13 12 11 10 9 8 7

Printed in Poland by Opolgraf

A catalogue record for this publication is available from the British Library

ISBN 978-1-108-40531-7 Student's Book
ISBN 978-1-108-40509-6 Student's Book A
ISBN 978-1-108-40923-0 Student's Book B
ISBN 978-1-108-40532-4 Student's Book with Practice Extra
ISBN 978-1-108-40510-2 Student's Book with Practice Extra A
ISBN 978-1-108-40925-4 Student's Book with Practice Extra B
ISBN 978-1-108-40901-8 Workbook with Audio
ISBN 978-1-108-40874-5 Workbook with Audio A
ISBN 978-1-108-41194-3 Workbook with Audio B
ISBN 978-1-108-40518-8 Teacher's Edition with Test Generator
ISBN 978-1-108-41071-7 Presentation Plus
ISBN 978-1-108-41204-9 Class Audio CDs
ISBN 978-1-108-40795-3 Video Resource Book with DVD
ISBN 978-1-108-41449-4 Full Contact with DVD
ISBN 978-1-108-41155-4 Full Contact A with DVD
ISBN 978-1-108-41417-3 Full Contact B with DVD

Additional resources for this publication at www.cambridge.org/evolve

Cambridge University Press has no responsibility for the persistence or accuracy of URLs for external or third-party internet websites referred to in this publication, and does not guarantee that any content on such websites is, or will remain, accurate or appropriate. Information regarding prices, travel timetables, and other factual information given in this work is correct at the time of first printing but Cambridge University Press does not guarantee the accuracy of such information thereafter.

CONTENTS

1.1   THIS IS ME!

1 VOCABULARY: Describing accomplishments

A   **Circle the words to complete the phrase. One phrase has two correct answers.**

1   break *a fear / (a record)*
2   face *a fear / a medal*
3   get *a business / a lot of likes*
4   have *a good joke / a sense of humor*
5   rise *to a challenge / a goal for myself*
6   run *a business / a marathon*
7   set *a goal for myself / pride in something*
8   take *a medal for something / pride in something*
9   tell *a goal for myself / a good joke*
10   win *a medal / a record*
11   work *with my hands / a business*

B   **Complete the sentences with phrases from exercise 1A.**

1   When you _____run a business_____ , you organize or control a business.
2   When you _____ , you say something to make people laugh.
3   When you _____ , you create something for your job.
4   When you _____ , you get a prize in a competition.
5   When you post something online that many people think is good, you _____ .
6   When you _____ , you feel good about something you have done.
7   When you _____ , you deal with something you are afraid of.
8   When you _____ , you deal with a difficult job or opportunity successfully.
9   When you _____ , you are involved in a really long race.
10   When you _____ , you do something faster or better than anyone else.
11   When you _____ , you decide something you want to do in the future.
12   When you _____ , you are able to understand funny things and to be funny yourself.

C   **Imagine you are in these situations. What might you say? Use the phrases from exercise 1A to write a sentence for each.**

1   **at a party:**   *Miranda, tell us a good joke.*
2   **at a job interview:** _____
3   **at a sporting event:** _____

2 GRAMMAR: Tense review (simple and continuous)

A **Some of the underlined verbs are not correct. Fix the mistakes.**

           went

1 I ~~was going~~ to a party last night. It <u>was</u> fun.

2 What <u>do</u> you <u>do</u> right now? <u>Are</u> you busy?

3 Jorge <u>has gotten</u> a job, but Rosa <u>has looked</u> for six months and <u>is</u> still <u>looking</u>.

4 <u>Have</u> you <u>heard</u> the news? Tony and Ana <u>have been getting</u> married.

5 I <u>talked</u> to Julia when you <u>called</u>. She <u>was telling</u> me a funny story.

B **Complete the paragraph with the correct form of the verbs in the box. Some verbs will be used more than once.**

~~be~~	get	(not) see	take	talk	wait	walk

There ¹ _____ *have been* _____ strange events in my neighborhood recently. I ² _____ down the street a couple of days ago when I ³ _____ a cow. Yes, that's right, a cow! You ⁴ _____ often _____ cows in the middle of a city. In fact, I ⁵ _____ never _____ one. But last Monday at 4:15 in the afternoon, there ⁶ _____ a cow in the middle of the road. Drivers ⁷ _____ out of their cars. A lot of people ⁸ _____ pictures. People in the neighborhood ⁹ _____ to each other about the cow ever since. We ¹⁰ _____ to see what the next strange event will be.

C **Write true sentences about you. Replace X with a word or phrase to complete each sentence.**

1 In my entire life, I / never / see / X

    In my entire life, I've never seen a cow on a street.

2 I / walk / down the street the other day when / X

    _____

3 You / often / (not) see / X / in my neighborhood

    _____

4 Once / I / X / but / I / never / X / it again

    _____

5 I / X / right now because I / X

    _____

6 I / try to / X / for a long time / but / I / still / X

    _____

1.2 THE RIGHT CANDIDATE

1 VOCABULARY: Describing key qualities

A **Check (✓) the correct underlined words. Correct the incorrect words.**

1 He is a very ~~responsibility~~ *responsible* person. ☐

2 She has the right <u>qualifications</u> for the job. ☑

3 He has a lot of <u>curious</u>. ☐

4 I hope to be very <u>success</u> in the future. ☐

5 I like their <u>independence</u>. ☐

6 You're not very <u>ambitious</u>, are you? ☐

7 I'm very <u>experience</u>. ☐

8 It's important to treat people <u>polite</u>. ☐

9 This job requires a lot of <u>creativity</u>. ☐

10 She doesn't have much <u>enthusiastic</u>. ☐

11 Thank you for your <u>truthfulness</u>. ☐

12 Are you <u>confident</u> when you speak English? ☐

2 GRAMMAR: Stative and dynamic verbs

A **Write S (stative verb) or D (dynamic verb).**

1 Are you being truthful?   D

2 We usually interview five people for every job.   _____

3 I take a photography class on Tuesday evenings.   _____

4 The report is very interesting.   _____

5 Do you know Lily?   _____

6 Why do they hate their job?   _____

7 I need some help.   _____

8 I'm thinking of changing jobs.   _____

B   Complete each pair of sentences with the stative and dynamic use of the verb in parentheses ( ).

1   (see)   a   Tom _____is seeing_____ the doctor. He'll be home soon.

b   I _____see_____ two people outside.

2   (have)   a   Melina _____ experience.

b   The doctor's in the cafeteria. She _____ lunch.

3   (think)   a   We _____ about moving to a bigger place.

b   What _____ you _____ of the class?

4   (smell)   a   He _____ the fish. Maybe there's something wrong with it.

b   Everything _____ delicious. Let's eat!

5   (weigh)   a   The suitcase _____ 22 kilos.

b   I don't know the price yet. The man _____ the meat now.

3   GRAMMAR AND VOCABULARY

A   **Complete the job reference for Alex Martinez. Use the correct form of the verbs in parentheses ( ). What qualities from exercise 1A does he have? Circle them.**

I [1] _____know_____ (know) Alex well. I [2] _____ (know) him for ten years. He [3] _____ (work) at the company for six. He is a responsible person and [4] _____ (take) his job very seriously. He is definitely qualified for the job. He [5] _____ (have) two degrees and many years of experience. He's ambitious and clearly [6] _____ (want) to be successful. He [7] _____ (set) goals for himself and then [8] _____ (do) the work to achieve them. He is curious and loves to learn new things. He [9] _____ (talk) to a lot of people who are different from him and [10] _____ (try) to learn from them. In fact, right now he [11] _____ (take) two classes at the local community college in different subjects. I'm not surprised that Alex [12] _____ (look) for a job with more responsibilities. His confidence is just another one of his excellent qualities. We will be sorry to lose him.

B   **Use the word prompts to write part of a job reference for someone you know. Replace X with a word or phrase to complete each sentence.**

1   She/He / work / at this job / X years

She has worked at this job for three years.

2   She/He / X / worker

_____

_____

3   Right now / she/he / X

_____

_____

4   Her/His / X / one of her/his excellent qualities

_____

_____

1.3 WE GO WAY BACK

1 FUNCTIONAL LANGUAGE: Making and responding to introductions

A **Complete the sentences. Match 1–7 in column A with a–g in column B.**

A

1 Do you … _____c_____
2 I don't think … _____
3 You're new … _____
4 Do you two know … _____
5 Have you … _____
6 Let me introduce you … _____
7 Is this your … _____

B

a here, right?
b met my assistant?
c know anyone here?
d first day?
e to a couple of people.
f we've met before.
g each other?

B **Put the conversation in the correct order.**

Jack   Yes, I just started this morning.   _____

Jack   It's nice to meet you, Sofia.   _____

Sofia   Hello. I don't think we've met before.   ___1___

Sofia   My name is Sofia.   _____

Sofia   It's nice to meet you, too. Is this your first day?   _____

Jack   No, we haven't met yet. I'm Jack.   _____

2 REAL-WORLD STRATEGY: Responding to an introduction

A **Complete the conversations. Use the words in the box.**

go	going	haven't	hi	I'm	love	met	see	~~sure~~	went

1 **Dan**   Have you met Sandra?

   Luis   I'm not _____sure_____ , but _____ , I'm Luis.

2 **Dan**   Do you know Sandra?

   Chris Yes, we _____ way back. We _____ to school together. How's it _____ , Sandra?

3 **Dan**   Have you met Sandra?

   Marta No, I _____ , but I'd _____ to. Hi, Sandra. _____ Marta.

4 **Dan**   Do you two know each other?

   Ruta   Yes, we _____ this morning! Nice to _____ you again, Sandra.

3 FUNCTIONAL LANGUAGE AND REAL-WORLD STRATEGY

A **Complete the conversation. Use the language you practiced in exercises 1A and 2A.**

1 **Armando** Hi. I don't think we've met before.
_____ You're new _____ here, right?

Clara _____ yesterday

Armando I'm Armando.

Clara Nice _____ . I'm Clara.

Armando Nice to meet you, too, Clara. Let me
_____ . Tom, this is Clara.

Tom Hey Clara! _____ ?

Armando _____ each other?

Clara Yeah, _____ yesterday.

2 **Sara** Is this your _____ ?
I'm Sara.

Rick Hi Sara. It's _____ .
I'm Rick.

Sara Do you _____ ?

Rick No, not yet.

Sara _____
to a couple of people. Zack, this is Rick.

Zack _____ , Rick.

Rick _____ , too.

B **Choose one of the following situations. Write a conversation introducing the people. Use the language you practiced in exercises 1 A and 2A.**

Situation 1: Marcel has just moved into your neighborhood. Introduce yourself.

Situation 2: Francesca is new to your class. Introduce her to some of your classmates.

A _____

_____

B _____

_____

A _____

_____

B _____

_____

1.4 FLIPPING YOUR JOB INTERVIEW

1 READING

A **Read the blog post. Then check (✓) the best title.**

1 Preparing for an interview? ☐

2 Getting the job you want! ☐

3 Dress for success! ☐

Blog   Share   Comment

You've finally gotten the interview you've wanted for months. Now you're busy preparing for the interview. You've researched the company and thought about the questions you want to ask.

What else is there? What you're going to wear. The way you look is very important. At the end of the interview, you want people to be talking about your experience, not your appearance.

What should you wear? Suits and ties for guys, and dresses for women? That's not always necessary. It depends on the type of job you're applying for.

Is it a job in the computer industry? You might not need a suit or a dress, but that doesn't mean you can go in a T-shirt and jeans. You need to look like you're going to work, not out for the night with friends. So, guys, put on a nice shirt and stylish pants. And, women, a nice sweater or blouse with a skirt or pants will be fine.

If you're interviewing for a finance job, you need to wear what people in the business world wear. That means a suit and tie for men and dresses or suits for women.

Dress for the job you want. Make sure your clothes are clean and ironed. Avoid wearing perfume or cologne, and don't wear too much makeup or jewelry.

Remember: If after the interview people are talking about your appearance, you probably won't hear from them again. So dress right and look good. Your career may depend on it.

B **READ FOR GIST** **Complete the statements. Use the phrases in the box.**

goes to a lot of job interviews	has interviewed people	buy clothes
is going to go to a job interview	get a job	interview people

1 The person who wrote the article is someone who _____.

2 The person who reads the article is someone who _____.

3 The purpose of the article is to help someone _____.

2 LISTENING

A 🔊 **1.01** **Listen to the conversation. Answer the questions.**

1 When is the man's interview? _____

2 Where has he applied for a job? _____

3 What should he wear? _____

4 What's the problem? _____

3 WRITING

A Read the comments in response to the blog post in exercise 1A. Underline the sentence that shows agreement. Circle the sentence that shows disagreement. Put a box around the sentences that show appreciation.

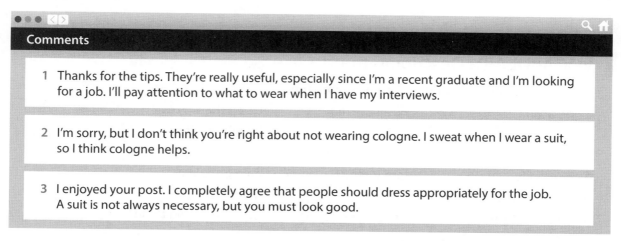

Comments

1 Thanks for the tips. They're really useful, especially since I'm a recent graduate and I'm looking for a job. I'll pay attention to what to wear when I have my interviews.

2 I'm sorry, but I don't think you're right about not wearing cologne. I sweat when I wear a suit, so I think cologne helps.

3 I enjoyed your post. I completely agree that people should dress appropriately for the job. A suit is not always necessary, but you must look good.

B Write two comments in response to the blog post in exercise 1A. In one comment, show appreciation and agree. In the second comment, disagree. Which comment reflects your true opinion?

_____

_____

_____

_____

_____

CHECK AND REVIEW

Read the statements. Can you do these things?

UNIT 1	Mark the boxes. ☑ I can do it. ? I am not sure. I can …	If you are not sure, go back to these pages in the Student's Book.
VOCABULARY	☐ use expressions to talk about personal achievements.	page 2
	☐ use nouns and adjectives to talk about key qualities employers look for.	page 4
GRAMMAR	☐ use a variety of simple and continuous verb forms.	page 3
	☐ use dynamic and stative verbs to talk about actions, habits, and states.	page 5
FUNCTIONAL LANGUAGE	☐ make introductions.	page 6
	☐ respond to an introduction.	page 7
SKILLS	☐ write a comment in response to a blog post.	page 9
	☐ agree, disagree, and show appreciation.	page 9

UNIT 2 — THE FUTURE OF FOOD

2.1 MENU WITH A MISSION

1 VOCABULARY: Describing trends

A Cross out the phrase that is different in meaning.

1 be a fad	be all the rage	~~be on the way out~~
2 be dated	be fashionable	be old-fashioned
3 come back in style	go out of fashion	lose popularity
4 be trendy	lose interest	gain popularity
5 be the next big thing	gain interest	go out of style
6 be on the way out	be the latest thing	be the next big thing

B Answer the questions about trends.

1 What is something you think is a fad?

In my opinion, long beards are a fad. I don't think they'll be popular next year.

2 What is a type of clothing you think is dated?

3 What is a type of music that is gaining popularity?

4 What is a type of music that is going out of style?

5 What type of diets are trendy right now?

6 What do you think will be the next big thing in fashion?

7 What is something that is all the rage right now?

8 What is something you think is old-fashioned?

2 GRAMMAR: Real conditionals

A Put the words in the correct order to make sentences.

1 the server / to waste / want / for a doggy bag / ask / don't / you / the food / if

If you don't want to waste the food, ask the server for a doggy bag. OR Ask the server for a doggy bag if you don't want to waste the food.

2 people won't / just a fad / for very long / if / do / it's / it

_____

_____

3 the chocolate pizza / like / if / have / you / to try / different kinds of food / you

_____

_____

4 to waste food / if / get worse / the problem / continue / will / we

_____

_____

5 on social media / everyone / something / trending / pays attention / if / is

_____

_____

6 expensive / a restaurant / if / it / gourmet food / usually / is / serves

_____

_____

B Complete the sentences. Use the words in parentheses ( ).

1 Fish _____is_____ (be) good for you if it _____isn't_____ (not / be) fried.

2 If we _____ (not / put) the meat in the fridge soon, it _____ (go) bad.

3 If you _____ (be) allergic to nuts, _____ (not / eat) the cake. It has nuts.

4 _____ (not / drink) coffee at night if you _____ (have) trouble falling asleep.

5 If you _____ (make) dinner tomorrow, I _____ (cook) it tonight.

6 _____ (not / go) to Heaven Gourmet if you _____ (want) a cheap meal. It's an expensive place.

C How can people waste less food, eat better, and save money? Write your ideas. Use *if*.

If you don't eat a lot of fast food, you'll have a healthier diet.

_____

_____

_____

_____

_____

_____

_____

_____

2.2 FOOD YOU FERMENT

1 VOCABULARY: Preparing food

A **Cross out the food that is in a different food group.**

1 ~~pineapple~~   garlic   mint
2 eggplant   tuna   zucchini
3 garlic   shrimp   tuna
4 cabbage   pineapple   zucchini
5 ginger   mint   zucchini

B **Complete the sentences with words from exercise 1A. More than one answer may be possible.**

1 Mariel likes to put a little bit of _____ in her tea.

2 Do you have a stick of gum or a breath mint? The pasta I had for lunch had too much _____ in it.

3 Jack went fishing last weekend and caught a 40-lb _____!

4 I have to remove the shells from these _____ before we cook them. Can you help me?

5 _____ is probably my favorite vegetable. I just love its purple color.

C **Complete the sentences. Use the words in the box.**

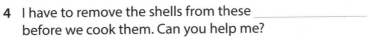

~~barbecue~~   boil   chop   fry   rinse   stir

1 If you ___barbecue___ a steak, you usually do it outside.
2 If you _____ fruit, you usually do it at the sink.
3 You need a spoon to _____ something.
4 If you _____ water, it becomes very hot.
5 You need a knife to _____ something.
6 You need oil to _____ something.

D **Answer the questions with your own information.**

1 Which foods in exercise 1A do you like?

_____

2 Are there foods in exercise 1A you have never tried?

_____

3 How often do you use the cooking methods in exercise 1C?

_____

4 What dish do you eat that uses a food from exercise 1A and a cooking method from exercise 1C?

_____

2 GRAMMAR: Clauses with *when, until, after*

A **Underline the event in each sentence that happens first.**

1 The sauce will change color when <u>you add the garlic</u>.
2 As soon as the food is done, we'll eat.
3 Before the water boils, put in the cabbage.
4 Add the zucchini after you fry the fish.
5 Cook the rice until there's no more water in the pot.
6 Once we finish lunch, we'll wash the dishes.

B **Combine the sentences. Use the time expression in parentheses ( ).**

1 I'm going to reserve a table. Then I'll tell you the time. (after)
   After I reserve a table, I'll tell you the time. OR *I'll tell you the time after I reserve a table.*

2 We'll get to the restaurant. Then we'll text you. (when)
   _____

3 We'll wait outside. You will arrive. (until)
   _____

4 The server will give us the menu. We'll order. (as soon as)
   _____

5 We'll pay the bill. Then we'll leave. (once)
   _____

6 We'll have dinner. Then we'll go to the movies. (before)
   _____

C **Write the correct form of the verb in parentheses ( ).**
Then complete the sentence with your own information.

1 When I _____*cook*_____ (cook) a big meal, _____*I'll invite all my friends*_____ .
2 After I _____ (get up) tomorrow morning, _____ .
3 I _____ (not go) to bed until _____ .
4 As soon as I _____ (have) some free time, _____ .
5 Once I _____ (save) enough money, _____ .

2.3 CAN I GET YOU A REFILL?

1 FUNCTIONAL LANGUAGE: Make, accept, and refuse offers

A **Change the underlined words in the sentences without changing the meaning. Use the words in the box.**

| I'm OK | ~~a refill~~ | care for | get | here |
| Awesome | offer | Oh | wonderful | want |

1 **A** Can I get you ~~another juice~~? *a refill*

   B <u>I'd better not</u>, thanks.

2 **A** Would you <u>like</u> some juice?

   B That'd be <u>great</u>.

3 **A** Can I <u>get</u> you another dessert?

   B <u>Yes</u>, that's great.

4 **A** Can I <u>have</u> another sausage, please?

   B Sure, <u>there</u> you go.

5 **A** Anyone else <u>care for</u> some cake? We have three different kinds.

   B <u>That's great</u>, I'll check it out.

2 REAL-WORLD STRATEGY: Acknowledge an acceptance

A **Read each conversation. Use the words below to complete each response.**

| back | got | right | sure |

1 **A** Can I offer you anything to drink?

   B Yes. Some coffee would be great.

   A I'll be right _____ with that.

2 **A** Would you pass me another cookie, please?

   B _____ thing.

3 **A** Is there any more iced tea?

   B Coming _____ up!

4 **A** Could I have a little more cake? It's delicious.

   B You _____ it!

B **Write two conversations. Speaker A makes an offer of food or drink. Speaker B accepts or refuses.**

1 **A** _____

   B _____

   A _____

2 **A** _____

   B _____

   A _____

FUNCTIONAL LANGUAGE AND REAL-WORLD STRATEGY

A **What do people often offer in these situations? Write three things.**

On an airplane	At a party	At a business meeting	At a restaurant
something to drink			
a snack			
a blanket			

B **Write conversations for each remaining situation in exercise 3A. Have people accept and refuse the offers.**

Flight attendant	Would you like something to drink?
Passenger	Yes, I'd love a glass of water.
Flight attendant	Coming right up!

Flight attendant	Can I get you a snack?
Passenger	I'd better not, thanks.

Flight attendant	Would you care for a blanket?
Passenger	That'd be wonderful.

Conversation 1

A _____

B _____

A _____

B _____

A _____

B _____

A _____

Conversation 2

A _____

B _____

A _____

B _____

A _____

B _____

A _____

Conversation 3

A _____

B _____

A _____

B _____

A _____

B _____

A _____

COOL FOOD

1 LISTENING

A 🔊 **2.01** **LISTEN FOR GIST** **Listen to a conversation between a man and a woman. Where do they decide to have lunch? Why?**

B 🔊 **2.01** **Listen again. Read the statements. Write _T_ (true) or _F_ (false). Correct the statements that are false.**

1 The woman is on a gluten-free diet because she wants to lose weight. _____

2 The woman has avoided eating things with gluten for the past six months. _____

3 The woman's family is also on a gluten-free diet. _____

4 The man and the woman are definitely going to lunch at Anna's. _____

2 READING

A **Read about the results of a survey about gluten-free diets. Circle the questions that the survey asked. Answer the questions you circle.**

> Gluten-free diets seem all the rage nowadays. You can see gluten-free foods in supermarkets and restaurants. News about the gluten-free diets of movie stars and professional athletes is all over social media. But what do people really know about gluten-free foods? Our survey results have some surprises.
>
> A majority of the people who responded said that being on a gluten-free diet improves physical or mental health. About 22 percent said they buy gluten-free products or try to avoid gluten.
>
> A quarter of the people in the survey thought that gluten-free foods have more nutrients than food with gluten. The truth is just the opposite.
>
> More than a third of the people interviewed thought that a gluten-free diet will help them lose weight. However, there is no research that proves this to be true. In fact, studies have shown that gluten-free diets can increase the risk of becoming overweight.

1 Does being on a gluten-free diet improve physical or mental health?

2 Do you buy gluten-free products or try to avoid gluten?

3 Is gluten-free food less expensive?

4 Do gluten-free foods have more nutrients than food with gluten?

5 Will a gluten-free diet help you lose weight?

3 WRITING

A Look at the charts from a college survey on what students drink. What trends do they show?

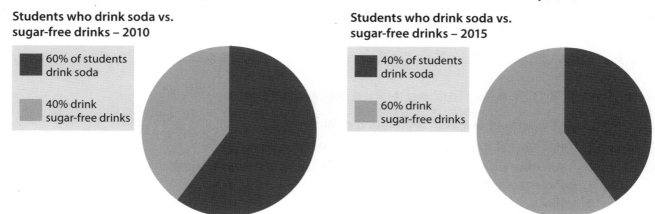

Students who drink soda vs. sugar-free drinks – 2010

- 60% of students drink soda
- 40% drink sugar-free drinks

Students who drink soda vs. sugar-free drinks – 2015

- 40% of students drink soda
- 60% drink sugar-free drinks

B Write a short report about the survey results. You can use the phrases below. Make sure you include numbers from the chart.

gain/lose popularity	be trendy	be on the way out	be a thing of the past
be the next big thing			

_____

_____

_____

_____

_____

CHECK AND REVIEW

Read the statements. Can you do these things?

UNIT 2	Mark the boxes. ☑ I can do it. ？ I am not sure.	If you are not sure, go back to these pages in the Student's Book.
	I can ...	
VOCABULARY	☐ use expressions to describe trends.	page 12
	☐ use the correct words to describe food preparation.	page 14
GRAMMAR	☐ use real conditionals.	page 13
	☐ refer to the future with time clauses using *when*, *until*, and *after*.	page 15
FUNCTIONAL LANGUAGE	☐ make, accept, and refuse offers.	page 16
	☐ acknowledge an acceptance	page 17
SKILLS	☐ write survey results.	page 19
	☐ reference numbers and statistics.	page 19

1 VOCABULARY: Talking about time and money

A **Circle the correct words to complete the sentences.**

1 If you <u>can't afford</u> to do something, you don't have the *time /(money)*.

2 If you have a good work-life <u>balance</u>, the amount of time you spend at work and doing things you enjoy are *about the same / very different*.

3 When you <u>boost</u> your chances of getting a job, you *decrease / increase* your chances.

4 The <u>cost of living</u> is the amount of money you need for *food, housing, and other basic things / parties, vacations, and other fun things*.

5 Your <u>lifestyle</u> is the *days of your life / way that you live*.

6 If you have a good <u>quality of life</u>, you have a lot of *money / satisfaction*.

7 Your <u>standard of living</u> is how much *money and comfort / money and family* you have.

8 If you <u>take a salary cut</u>, your salary goes *down / up*.

9 If something is <u>time well-spent</u>, it *takes a lot of time / is a good use of time*.

10 If you <u>trade</u> something, you *buy / exchange* it.

11 If you <u>value</u> something, it is *expensive / important to you*.

12 If something is <u>worth it</u>, it is difficult but *cheap / useful*.

B **Complete the sentences with your own information.**

1 I can't afford to _____ *move to a nicer place* _____ right now.

2 The thing I like most about my lifestyle is _____
_____ .

3 You know you don't have a good work-life balance when _____
_____ .

4 I would like to boost my chances of _____
_____ .

5 What I value most of all is _____
_____

6 It is time well-spent when I _____
_____ .

7 It's worth it to take a salary cut _____
_____ .

8 In order to have a good quality of life, it is important to _____
_____ .

2 GRAMMAR: *too* and *enough*

A Complete the sentences with *too* or *enough*. Use the words in the box.

| close | ~~experienced~~ | free time | money | slow | small |

1 Jorge's too inexperienced for the job. He isn't _____experienced enough_____ .
2 The job is too far from my home. It isn't _____ .
3 Lina isn't quick enough. She's _____ .
4 I work too many hours. I don't have _____ .
5 My salary is too low. I don't make _____ .
6 The office isn't big enough. It's _____ .

B Write sentences. Use the words in parentheses ( ) with *(not) too, too much, too many,* or *enough,* and the infinitive.

1 I want to go to the beach, but it's only 63° outside. (cold)
   It's too cold to go to the beach.

2 Ramón can't go to the club. He isn't 21 yet. (old)
   _____

3 Olga is tired after work, but she still cooks dinner. (tired)
   _____

4 Isabelle wants to take a long vacation, but she has only five vacation days. (time off)
   _____

5 Manuel can't go out for lunch. He's finishing a report. (busy)
   _____

6 It costs $20 to enter the museum. Trevor only has $15. (money)
   _____

C Write sentences that are true for you. Use *enough, too, too much,* or *too many.*

1 I / spend / time studying
   I spend too much time studying. OR I don't spend enough time studying.

2 I / have / things to do today
   _____

3 I / make / money
   _____

4 I / get / texts every day
   _____

5 My neighborhood / be / lively / at night
   _____

6 I / have / friends on social media
   _____

7 I / work / hard
   _____

THE PRICE OF A COFFEE

1 VOCABULARY: Talking about prices and value

A Complete the chart. Write each verb under the correct preposition.

charge	come up	depend	have an effect
invest	rely	make the most	pay a fair price
play an important role	suggest a price	take advantage	treat myself

for	on	of
charge		

in	to	with

B Complete the sentences with the verbs and prepositions in exercise 1A.

1 You should _____make the most of_____ the beautiful weather today. It's going to rain tomorrow.

2 Prices _____ what people are willing to pay.

3 Drinking too much coffee _____ my ability to sleep at night.

4 After a bad day, I _____ a bowl of ice cream.

5 Our guests can _____ many facilities at the hotel, such as restaurants, meeting rooms, and workout rooms.

6 I am willing to _____ food, but I think $12 for a sandwich is too much.

7 You can _____ the service at the restaurant. It's always fast.

8 To be successful, businesses need to _____ new ideas on a regular basis.

9 Should I _____ Sam's business? I'll make money if it's successful.

10 I'll never go back to that restaurant. They _____ a glass of water!

C Use at least three of the phrases in exercise 1A to write about shopping.

The last time I went shopping, the cashier forgot to charge me
for two things.

_____

_____

_____

_____

_____

_____

_____

2 GRAMMAR: Modifying comparisons

A Compare the bakeries below. Use the words in parentheses ( ) and *a bit, a little, much, a lot, more, way more,* or *by far.*

	Bob's Bakery	Crazy 4 Cake	Sweet Surprises
Price for cakes	$15	$25	$12
Busy times	11 a.m.–3 p.m.	all day	12 p.m.–2 p.m.
Likes	255	765	450
In business since	1952	2008	2010

1 Crazy 4 Cake has been open _____ *a little longer* _____ than Sweet Surprises. Of the three, Bob's Bakery has been open _____ . (long)

2 Crazy 4 Cake is _____ , but Bob's Bakery is _____ than Sweet Surprises. (expensive)

3 Sweet Surprises is _____ than Bob's Bakery, but Crazy 4 Cake is _____ . (popular)

4 Crazy 4 Cake is _____ of the three. Bob's Bakery is _____ than Sweet Surprises. (busy)

B Complete the sentences with *as … as* and *almost, nearly, nowhere near,* or *just.*

1 The pizza at Arturo's is much better than the pizza at Gina's.
Gina's pizza is _____ *not nearly as good as* _____ Arturo's.

2 The servers at Gina's are a little friendlier than the servers at Arturo's.
Arturo's servers are _____ Gina's are.

3 The seats at Gina's are really comfortable. Arturo's seats aren't comfortable at all.
Arturo's seats are _____ Gina's are.

4 Arturo's and Gina's are big. They both have 25 tables.
Gina's is _____ Arturo's is.

5 Gina's and Arturo's are new. Gina's opened in June of 2017. Arturo's opened six months later.
Gina's is _____ Arturo's is.

C Write true sentences about yourself. Replace X and Y with a word or phrase to complete each sentence.

1 X / by far / exciting / thing / I've ever seen.
The circus is by far the most exciting thing I've ever seen.

2 X / by far / good / gift / I've ever gotten.
_____

3 X / nowhere near / tasty / Y
_____

4 X / way / easy / Y
_____

5 X / a bit / expensive / Y
_____

6 X / just / intelligent / Y
_____

I'M SO SORRY!

1 FUNCTIONAL LANGUAGE: Apologize for damaging something

A **Complete the conversation. Use the words in the box.**

can't	didn't	don't	dumbest	how	so	~~sorry~~	what

Martin I'm really ¹_____sorry_____, but I just did the ²_____ thing.

Althea Oh no, ³_____ tell me something happened to my car. Did someone steal it?

Martin No, no. The car's outside. It's just that I had a small accident. You'll never guess ⁴_____ I did.

Althea What happened?

Martin I was parking the car and hit a tree. I can't tell you ⁵_____ sorry I am.

Althea A tree?

Martin I know. I ⁶_____ believe I ⁷_____ see it. I am ⁸_____ sorry. I'll pay for the damage.

Althea Let me call the insurance company and see if they'll pay. But first, let me see the car.

2 REAL-WORLD STRATEGY: Responding to an apology

A **Respond to the apologies. Put the words in the correct order.**

1 **Glen**   I'm so sorry I was late for the meeting.
    Andy   deal / it's / big / really / no

   _____

2 **Delcy**   I can't believe I forgot your birthday.
    Nate   over / don't / yourself / it / beat / up

   _____
   _____

3 **Ron**   I'm really sorry I didn't pick you up on time.
    Hee-an   end / the / the / not / world / it's / of

   _____
   _____

FUNCTIONAL LANGUAGE AND REAL-WORLD STRATEGY

A **Write a conversation for each situation. Use the language you practiced in exercises 1A and 2A.**

1 Victor lost Daria's book. He left it on the train. Daria doesn't want him to feel bad about it.

Victor Daria, I can't believe I did this but …

Daria Oh no, what?

Victor I left your book on the train. I can't tell you how sorry I am.

Daria It's just a book. Don't beat yourself up over it.

2 Keiko forgot about a meeting. She didn't put it on her calendar. Al doesn't want her to feel bad about it.

Keiko _____

Al _____

Keiko _____

Al _____

3 Joao texted Max the wrong directions, and Max got lost. Max doesn't want him to feel bad about it.

Joao _____

Max _____

Joao _____

Max _____

4 Alex is out of town. His friend Lin is staying at his apartment. Lin calls Alex to tell him something has happened and to apologize. Alex thinks Lin is going to tell him he broke the TV.

Lin _____

Alex _____

Lin _____

Alex _____

5 Hector says he broke one of Alice's good glasses. Alice doesn't want him to feel bad about it.

Hector _____

Alice _____

Hector _____

Alice _____

EPIC SHOPPING FAILS

1 READING

A **Read the blog post about shopping. Is the blogger writing about shopping online or in a store?**

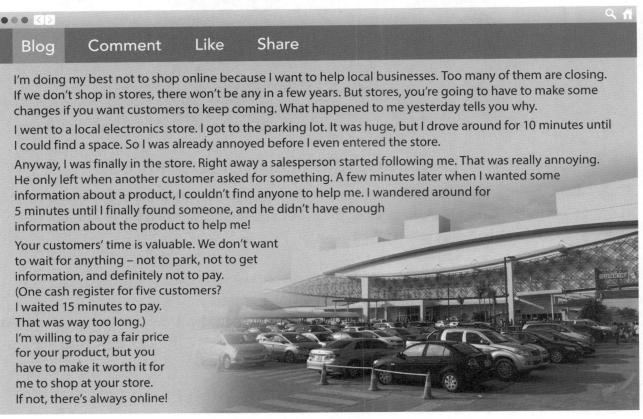

Blog   Comment   Like   Share

I'm doing my best not to shop online because I want to help local businesses. Too many of them are closing. If we don't shop in stores, there won't be any in a few years. But stores, you're going to have to make some changes if you want customers to keep coming. What happened to me yesterday tells you why.

I went to a local electronics store. I got to the parking lot. It was huge, but I drove around for 10 minutes until I could find a space. So I was already annoyed before I even entered the store.

Anyway, I was finally in the store. Right away a salesperson started following me. That was really annoying. He only left when another customer asked for something. A few minutes later when I wanted some information about a product, I couldn't find anyone to help me. I wandered around for 5 minutes until I finally found someone, and he didn't have enough information about the product to help me!

Your customers' time is valuable. We don't want to wait for anything – not to park, not to get information, and definitely not to pay. (One cash register for five customers? I waited 15 minutes to pay. That was way too long.) I'm willing to pay a fair price for your product, but you have to make it worth it for me to shop at your store. If not, there's always online!

B **READ FOR DETAIL** **Read the post again. Answer the questions.**

1 What does the blogger say about the parking lot?
   a It was too small.   b It was too full.

2 Why wasn't the salesperson helpful?
   a He didn't know about the product.   b He was rude.

3 What other problem did the blogger have?
   a She had to wait too long to pay.   b The store didn't have the product she wanted.

2 LISTENING

A 🔊 **3.01** **Listen to the conversation. Answer the questions.**

1 What kind of business does the woman work at? _____

2 Who gives her problems at work? _____

3 What did the Milk Lady do? _____

4 Why can't the woman fix the problem? _____

3 WRITING

A Read the store review. Underline the sentence that shows the reviewer's feeling. Circle the positive and negative features of the store. Put a box around the sentence that gives a recommendation.

> ● ● ● ◁ ▷　　　　　　　　　　　　　　　　　　　🔍 🏠
>
> **Store review**
>
> I highly recommend ProSports. I recently bought a tennis racket there. It's an excellent store with a wide variety of products and great prices. I couldn't find anything cheaper online. My only complaint is that there wasn't enough staff. Everyone was very friendly and knew a lot about the products, but there wasn't enough staff to take care of all the customers. Maybe that was because too many people know that ProSports is such a great store. It was my first time there. I'd definitely go back.

B Think of a store you have been to recently. Write a short review of the store.

_____

_____

_____

_____

_____

_____

_____

_____

_____

CHECK AND REVIEW

Read the statements. Can you do these things?

UNIT 3	Mark the boxes. ☑ I can do it. ❓ I am not sure. I can …		If you are not sure, go back to these pages in the Student's Book.
VOCABULARY	☐	use expressions to talk about time and money.	page 22
	☐	use verb phrases to talk about prices and value.	page 24
GRAMMAR	☐	use (*not*) *too* and (*not*) *enough* to talk about quantity.	page 23
	☐	use modifiers in comparisons.	page 25
FUNCTIONAL LANGUAGE	☐	apologize for damaging something.	page 26
	☐	respond to an apology.	page 27
SKILLS	☐	write a product review.	page 29
	☐	describe feelings and give recommendations.	page 29

1 VOCABULARY: Talking about advertising

A **Complete the sentences with words in the box.**

advertise	ad/advertisement	brands	commercials	fashion statement
logo	merchandise	merchandising	products	slogan
~~sponsor (n.)~~	sponsor (v.)	status symbols		

1 Al's Pizza pays to support our basketball team. They are our _____sponsor_____ . We have their _____ – "Best pizza in town!" – on our jerseys.

2 Louisa wears bright colors to make a _____ .

3 Dave's business was not doing well, so he decided to _____ on TV. He also hired an artist to design a new _____ for his business.

4 Have you seen the _____ for that new TV show? It looks really funny.

5 _____ from famous _____ , like Gucci and Prada, are often more expensive because they are _____ .

6 Disney makes a lot of its profits from _____ . The company charges other companies to put its characters on their products.

7 Many websites make money by hosting _____ for other companies and products.

8 Many companies will _____ a local charity or a sports team because they know it is good for their reputation.

9 The football stadium has a store inside that sells the team's _____ .

2 GRAMMAR: Modals of speculation

A **Circle the correct words.**

1 The fans are going to their seats. They *can't* / *must* have tickets.

2 Val was in second place in the race last time. She *might* / *must* win this time.

3 Andreas always wears a Santos jersey. He *could* / *must* like the team.

4 There's a man talking to the players. He *must* / *could* be the coach. Or maybe he's the referee.

5 Some fans are leaving the game early. They *can't* / *might* be bored.

6 Nobody is wearing a jacket. It *can't* / *could* be cold.

B **Complete the conversations. Use** *could*, *might*, *must*, **or** *can't* **and the verb in parentheses ( ).**

1 A Does Victor know Eve?

  B He _____must know_____ (know) her. They're taking the same class.

2 A Are there tickets available for tomorrow's game?

  B There _____ (be) tickets left. Let's look online and see.

3 A That's Marisol's brother.

  B He _____ (be) Marisol's brother. Everyone in her family is tall, and he's very short.

4 A Does Natalia like soccer?

  B She _____ (like) it. She talks about it all the time.

5 A We have a meeting tomorrow, right?

  B We _____ (have) a meeting. Mark hasn't decided yet.

6 A Tom's at the door.

  B Tom _____ (be) at the door. He's at work.

3 GRAMMAR AND VOCABULARY

A **Write an explanation for each fact. Use modals of speculation and the words in the box or your own ideas.**

be rich	be well known	help people to remember
help to sell merchandise	~~look good~~	make (someone) feel special

1 Christine likes to make a fashion statement with her choice of clothes.

  It might be important for her to look good.

2 Nike has had the slogan "Just do it" for years.

  _____

  _____

3 People like to buy cool brands.

  _____

  _____

4 Commercials with music are more successful than commercials without music.

  _____

  _____

5 People buy Rolex watches because they are a status symbol.

  _____

  _____

6 A good logo is very important for a company.

  _____

  _____

VIRAL STORIES

1 VOCABULARY: Talking about people in the media

A **Look at the clues and complete the crossword.**

ACROSS

2 This person gets paid to wear the latest designs.
5 This word has a similar meaning to *performer*.
7 Beyonce is more than just a singer. She's a cultural …
8 This person plays music so people can dance.
9 This person is paid to tell jokes.
10 This is someone who is famous.

DOWN

1 This word has a similar meaning to *director*.
3 This is someone who is brave or who people admire.
4 This person makes new fashions.
6 At a concert, these are the people in the crowd.

2 GRAMMAR: Subject and object relative clauses

A **Write *where, which, who, that,* or – (if a relative pronoun is not necessary).**

1 I like stores ___that___ OR ___which___ have a lot of different products.
2 I never go to restaurants _____ I have to wait.
3 My friends _____ live far away text me all the time.
4 I share all the photos _____ I take with friends and family.
5 I don't like problems _____ keep me awake at night.
6 I don't give money to people _____ I don't know.
7 I would like to be someone _____ other people admire.

B **Combine the sentences. Use relative pronouns where necessary.**

1 Some stories are unbelievable. The stories go viral.
   Some stories that go viral are unbelievable.

2 The stories are about animals. I like those stories the most.
   The stories that I like the most are about animals.

3 People must have a lot of free time. These people watch a lot of videos.

4 People share stories. They think the stories are funny.

5 There's a video with a cat. The cat is playing the piano.

6 Once I saw a video of a house. Fifty cats lived in the house.

7 One great video still makes me laugh. I saw the video last year.

8 My friends thought it was funny, too. My friends saw the video.

3 GRAMMAR AND VOCABULARY

A **Write sentences that are true for you. Use relative pronouns where necessary.**

1 performers / perform online / always / get / a lot of likes
   Performers who perform online don't always get a lot of likes. OR *Performers who perform online always get a lot of likes.*

2 a podcaster / become / a celebrity / always / make / a lot of money

3 the icons / I / admire / be / all from my country

4 it / be / fun / to be in an audience / I / don't know anyone

5 the photos / go viral / be / always / photos of heroes

6 the clothes / I / buy / be / usually / by famous designers

29

THAT'S A GOOD POINT, BUT ...

1 FUNCTIONAL LANGUAGE: Exchanging opinions

A **Match the columns to complete the conversations.**

1 I really think professional athletes are paid too much. _____

2 I find it very unfair that women athletes earn less than men. _____

3 I don't really think it's better to watch sports live than on TV. _____

4 High school students should focus on their studies, not on sports. _____

5 Don't you think we expect too much from professional athletes? _____

a As I see it, they have a responsibility to be good role models. _____

b Yes, absolutely. There's no reason they should earn less. _____

c It's not so much that it's better. It's just different. _____

d Just a second. Pro athletes train really hard. They earn their salaries. _____

e OK, that's a good point, but high school sports aren't all bad. _____

B **Complete the conversation with the expressions in the box.**

I really think	just a second	as I see it	that's a good point	I found it
it's just that	that's true but	it's not so much that		

Derek   So, Elisa, what did you think of the book?

Elisa   I hated it. [1] _____ really boring.

Derek   Yeah, me too. [2] _____ it's the worst book we've read this year.

Tae-hyun   Now, [3] _____ . I liked it. It was so different from the stuff we usually read.

Elisa   [4] _____ , but being different doesn't mean it was good.

Tae-hyun   Well, Derek, I'm surprised you didn't like it. You usually love science fiction.

Derek   [5] _____ this book was more about the relationship between the two main characters – not really about the space travel. [6] _____ , this book was really more of a love story.

Tae-hyun   [7] _____ it's a love story, [8] _____ love is an important part of the story. I still think it's science fiction.

2 REAL-WORLD STRATEGY: Making opinions more emphatic

A **Correct the mistakes in the responses.**

1 **A** The Aztecs are the best team in the league.

   B Sorry, I can't disagree more!

2 **A** Romantic comedies are always so dumb.

   B That's not true in all!

3 **A** Manu Ginobili wasn't that great of a basketball player.

   B You have it wrong!

3 FUNCTIONAL LANGUAGE AND REAL-WORLD STRATEGY

A Read the conversation. Circle the expressions that discuss or exchange opinions. Underline the expressions that make opinions more emphatic.

A What are you doing?

B Just reading one of those online gossip sites.

A Why do you read that trash?

B Now just a second, there's a lot of really good celebrity news here.

A As I see it, it's mostly just lies. Hardly any of that stuff is true.

B That's not true at all. When Khloe Kardashian had her baby, where do you think I read about it? On this site. That wasn't made up, was it?

A OK, that's true, but it's still just gossip. It's not news – it doesn't have any effect on your life.

B You have it all wrong. I don't read this site for news. I read it to be entertained. Not every news site has to be serious.

A It's not so much that I think all news has to be serious, it's just that I think the stories on this site are so dumb. I don't even find it entertaining.

B Well I couldn't disagree more. Now, if you don't mind, I going to finish reading this article.

B Read Yusef's and Abigail's opinions on camping. Then write a conversation between Yusef and Abigail about camping. Use expressions to discuss and exchange opinions, and to make opinions more emphatic.

Yusef I love camping! I love getting out of the city and away from all the noise. It's just a lot of fun. You get to sleep outside and see the stars, cook over a fire, and maybe see some wildlife. It's really my favorite way to spend a weekend.	**Abigail** Camping is the worst! You have to sleep outside, and there are bugs everywhere. And I'm constantly scared that I'll see a bear or some other wild animal. I guess cooking over a fire is OK, but I can barbeque in my backyard!

Yusef _____

Abigail _____

Yusef _____

Abigail _____

Yusef _____

Abigail _____

Yusef _____

Abigail _____

4.4 BUILDING A BRAND

1 LISTENING

A 🔊 **4.01** **LISTEN FOR GIST** **Listen to the podcast. What does the speaker talk about?**

B 🔊 **4.01** **LISTEN FOR DETAILS** **Listen again. Answer the questions. Write _Y_ (yes) or _N_ (no).**

1 Does the speaker say that every company can be successful internationally? _____

2 Should a company that does not have enough customers at home sell abroad? _____

3 Could a company fail abroad if it doesn't understand the culture of a country? _____

4 Is it important for companies to work with people from other countries? _____

2 READING

A **Read the article. Write the missing information.**

Red Bull is an example of an international success story. The brand has become so popular that people don't even realize where the drink comes from. They think it is either from their country or the United States. Very few people know that Red Bull is Austrian.

Actually, Red Bull is even more international. The owner, Dietrich Mateschitz, got the idea for Red Bull from an energy drink in Thailand. It was called Krating Daeng, which is Thai for "red bull." Dietrich Mateschitz discovered Krating Daeng during a trip to Asia in 1982. He went into business with Chaleo Yoovidhya, the creator of the Thai drink. Mateschitz made some changes to the flavor and started selling Red Bull in Austria in 1987.

Today Red Bull is sold around the world. It is not only a drink. With its slogan "Red Bull gives you wings," it has become a lifestyle icon.

1 Red Bull is an _____ company.

2 The name of the owner is _____ .

3 The owner became interested in Red Bull when he was in _____ .

4 _Krating Daeng_ means _____ .

5 Chaleo Yoovidhya was the person _____ .

3 WRITING

A **Read the social media comment. Underline the five words and phrases that mean "because (of)" and "so."**

●●● <>   🔍 🏠

👤   Add comment   Like   Share

Global brands are everywhere these days. As a result, some local companies are closing. This is a very serious problem. Due to the fact that businesses are closing, people are losing their jobs. As they no longer have jobs, they buy less. That affects other companies. Consequently, more people lose their jobs. What can we do about this? We should try to buy local brands. If we have to pay a little more, we should do that. It will save so many jobs. We can't keep global brands out of our country. Thanks to the Internet, new products can become international brands very quickly. But we can think about our country's workers when we choose what to buy.

B **Write a comment about one of the topics in the box. Use at least three of the words or phrases you underlined in exercise 3A.**

> your opinion about buying global brands   a brand you always buy
> a brand you used to like that no longer exists

_____

_____

_____

_____

_____

CHECK AND REVIEW

Read the statements. Can you do these things?

UNIT 4	Mark the boxes. ☑ I can do it. ? I am not sure. I can ...	If you are not sure, go back to these pages in the Student's Book.
VOCABULARY	☐ describe different features of ads and the techniques used.	page 34
	☐ talk about celebrities and viral news.	page 36
GRAMMAR	☐ make speculations.	page 35
	☐ use pronouns in relative clauses.	page 37
FUNCTIONAL LANGUAGE	☐ give, respond to, and critique opinions.	page 38
	☐ make opinions more emphatic.	page 39
SKILLS	☐ write a comment about local and global brands.	page 41
	☐ write about cause and effect.	page 41

1 VOCABULARY: Describing stories

A **Complete the sentences with words from the box.
There may be more than one answer.**

~~family saga~~	horror story	personal tragedy
tall tale	feel-good story	human interest story
mystery	hard-luck story	love story
success story	tear jerker	

1 This kind of story is long and is about many different family members and events. _____family saga_____

2 In this kind of story, the main character faces death, injury, or great difficulties. _____

3 In this kind of story, we feel sorry for the problems someone has. _____

4 This kind of story is about two people who develop strong positive feelings for each other.
_____

5 This kind of story is about someone who has a lot of achievements. _____

6 This kind of story is about something strange or unusual that happened. _____

7 In this kind of story, someone tells us something he or she says is true, but that is hard to believe. _____

8 This kind of story is intended to make us feel sorry for the person who tells the story. _____

9 This kind of story gives people happy feelings about life. _____

10 This kind of story surprises people and makes them afraid. _____

11 In this kind of story we connect emotionally with a person's problems, concerns or achievements. _____

2 GRAMMAR: Past perfect

A **Match sentences 1–6 with the sentences in the box. Then underline the events that happened first.**

~~I hadn't studied.~~	He'd missed his flight.	I had lost it.
He woke up in the hospital.	The party was over.	The movie had ended.

1 I failed the exam. _____I hadn't studied._____

2 The money wasn't in my pocket. _____

3 He'd had an accident. _____

4 He arrived 10 minutes late. _____

5 I left the theater. _____

6 Everyone had left. _____

B   Complete the paragraph below. Use the past perfect form of the words in the box.

| be | ~~break~~ | open | put | take | throw |

Julio and Marcella came home late from a party one evening. They were shocked to see that one of the living room windows was broken. Someone [1]____had broken____ the glass. The back door was unlocked. Someone [2]_____ the door. The dog was in the basement. Someone [3]_____ the dog there. They found their books and important papers on the floor. Someone [4]_____ them off the desk. Their laptops were gone. Someone [5]_____ them. Julio and Marcella called the police because they [6]_____ robbed.

3   GRAMMAR AND VOCABULARY

A   Read the story below. Put the events in the correct order. Then decide: Is it a personal tragedy, a feel-good story, or a family saga?

_____   His parents are very worried.
___1___   A young boy goes fishing with his dog.
_____   The boy is missing for 12 hours.
_____   After a few hours, the boy gets lost.
_____   The parents are very happy.
_____   Luckily, the dog helps him find his way home again.

B   Complete the story from exercise 3A. Use the simple past, past continuous, and past perfect.

A young boy had gone fishing with his dog. After a few hours, _____

_____

_____

_____

_____

_____

_____

_____

1 VOCABULARY: Making and breaking plans

A **Complete the phrasal verbs with *ahead, down, out, forward,* or *together*.**

Jess Hi, Leo. What happened last night? We all got ¹ ___together___ at the new pizza place in town. We thought you were coming but then we gave ² _____ on you.

Leo Yeah, I know. Sorry I let you ³ _____ . I don't mean to make ⁴ _____ excuses, but yesterday was just the worst day. First, my car was stolen. I ended ⁵ _____ taking three buses to Gina's place. Then she split ⁶ _____ with me.

Jess Really? I'm so sorry. That's terrible. A day like that could mess ⁷ _____ your whole month.

Leo Thanks Jess. Right now I'm just trying to stay positive. Anyway, I'm headed to lunch now. Should I wait for you or go ⁸ _____ without you?

Jess Don't wait. I'm going to be held ⁹ _____ here a little longer. Do you want to do something later today, maybe to cheer you ¹⁰ _____ ?

Leo Thanks, but tonight I'm going to hang ¹¹ _____ with my family. And I also feel like I'm getting a cold.

Jess Well, I'm sure you're looking ¹² _____ to your vacation at least. Vacations always make me feel better.

Leo Definitely. After all this it will be nice to get away for a couple of days. But let's get ¹³ _____ when I'm back.

2 GRAMMAR: *was/were going to; was/were supposed to*

A **Check (✓) the correct sentences.**

1 I was going call you, but I forgot. ☐

2 We were going to leave at 8, but we left at 9. ☑

3 The kids were suppose to get out of school an hour ago. Where are they? ☐

4 You going to pay me last week. I'm still waiting for the money. ☐

5 It supposed to rain today, but it's a beautiful day. ☐

6 Was I supposed to meet Professor Yu yesterday? I can't remember. ☐

B **Now correct the incorrect sentences from exercise 2A.**

I was going to call you, but I forgot.

_____

_____

_____

_____

_____

_____

C **Manuel checked the things he did last week. Complete the sentences about the things he did <u>not</u> do. Use was/were going to in 1–3 and was/were supposed to in 4–6.**

12:00 PM

Reminders

buy a new jacket
play tennis with Sam
sign up for an art
  class
get my car fixed ✓
meet Ali for dinner
see Dr. Garcia ✓
send a gift to Rena
visit Aunt Rita

1 _He was going to buy a new jacket_ , but he didn't.
2 _____ , but he didn't.
3 _____ , but he didn't.
4 _____ , but he didn't.
5 _____ , but he didn't.
6 _____ , but he didn't.

3 GRAMMAR AND VOCABULARY

A **Complete the sentences. Use the words in parentheses ( ) and the correct form of the phrasal verbs in the box.**

cheer up	get together	go ahead	~~hang out~~
make up	mess up	split up	

1 Luis and his friends _____ were going to hang out _____ (going to) at the mall last night, but the mall closed early.

2 I _____ (going to) with my friends for a movie, but I was held up.

3 The band _____ (going to) after their June concert, but they played together for one more year.

4 Charlie wasn't feeling well, but his parents _____ (going to) with the party. Then they changed their minds.

5 The party _____ (supposed to) Elisa, but it didn't. She was still sad.

6 Jessica _____ (going to) an excuse for missing the test. But in the end she told the truth.

7 Updating the operating system _____ (not supposed to) my phone, but it sure did. It won't even turn on now!

5.3 THERE MUST BE A MISTAKE!

1 FUNCTIONAL LANGUAGE: Reacting to bad news

A Read the reactions to a problem. Circle the correct words. Then label each sentence *reaction*, *escalation*, or *resolution*.

1 *There is /* (*Is there*) someone (*else*) */ more* I can speak to about this, please?   *escalation*

2 I *'m not / don't* get it.   _____

3 I'm just glad *that / that's* settled.   _____

4 *You can / Can you* check again, please?   _____

5 *That's / This is* quite all right.   _____

6 *Will / Would* you mind *take / taking* another look?   _____

7 I don't *get / understand*.   _____

8 There *can / must* be something you *can / must* do.   _____

9 There *might / must* be a */ some* kind of mistake.   _____

10 I *like / 'd like* to speak to *manager / the manager*, please.   _____

2 REAL-WORLD STRATEGY: Accepting bad news

A Put the words in order to complete the responses.

1 **Salesperson** I can't lower the price of the car.

   You   that's not / to hear / but / what / can you / do / I hoped / what

   _____ ?

2 **Server** I'm sorry, but there's no more chicken soup today.

   You   it / it / what / is / well / is

   _____ .

3 **Manager** You can't leave work early today.

   You   life / well / that's

   _____ .

4 **Dry cleaner** I'm sorry, but your jacket isn't ready yet.

   You   too / that's / bad

   _____

   _____

   _____

3 FUNCTIONAL LANGUAGE AND REAL-WORLD STRATEGY

A **Jason is in a store and is speaking to Alma at the cash register. Put the sentences in the correct order.**

Alma	The shirt is $50. It's $35 if you pay in cash.	___
Alma	The sign says $35. Then in small letters it says "Cash."	___
Jason	Here's my credit card for the shirt. It's $35, right?	1
Jason	There must be some kind of mistake. The sign says $35.	___
Alma	The manager is busy. How about I give you this $15 tie for only $5?	___
Jason	That's not right. Is there someone else I can speak to about this, please?	___
Jason	Well, OK. I've never heard of a credit card difference in price, but I'm glad it's settled. Thanks.	___

B **Read the situation. Then complete the conversation using the expressions from exercises 1A and 2A.**

Situation: Arturo lost his credit card yesterday. Today he checked online and noticed a lot of new charges on his credit card. He calls the credit card company to ask them to remove the charges and cancel his card.

Credit card worker	Max One credit card. How may I help you?
Arturo	Hi. I lost my credit card yesterday, and today there are some charges on my card that I didn't make. I'd like to have those charges removed and have my credit card canceled.
Credit card worker	Well, I can cancel your credit card, but I can't remove the charges, sir.
Arturo	_____
Credit card worker	I'm sorry sir, but there isn't. You will be responsible for those charges.
Arturo	_____
Credit card worker	Of course, sir. I'll transfer you right now.
Manager	Hello sir. How can I help you?
Arturo	Well, I'm trying to get some charges removed from my credit card account. I lost my card yesterday, and I guess someone else found it and used it.
Manager	I'm sorry to hear that. But since you didn't report your card as lost yesterday, I can't totally remove the charges. But I can reduce them by 50%.
Arturo	_____ .

THE PERFECT APOLOGY?

1 READING

A **Read the blog post about apologies. Does the writer think apologies matter a little or a lot? How do you know?**

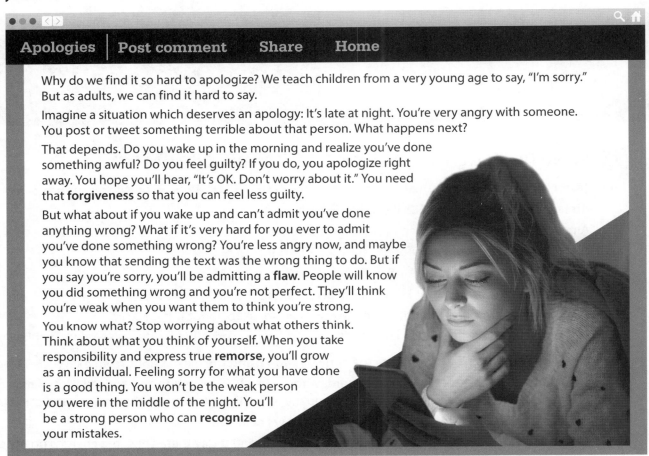

Apologies | Post comment | Share | Home

Why do we find it so hard to apologize? We teach children from a very young age to say, "I'm sorry." But as adults, we can find it hard to say.

Imagine a situation which deserves an apology: It's late at night. You're very angry with someone. You post or tweet something terrible about that person. What happens next?

That depends. Do you wake up in the morning and realize you've done something awful? Do you feel guilty? If you do, you apologize right away. You hope you'll hear, "It's OK. Don't worry about it." You need that **forgiveness** so that you can feel less guilty.

But what about if you wake up and can't admit you've done anything wrong? What if it's very hard for you ever to admit you've done something wrong? You're less angry now, and maybe you know that sending the text was the wrong thing to do. But if you say you're sorry, you'll be admitting a **flaw**. People will know you did something wrong and you're not perfect. They'll think you're weak when you want them to think you're strong.

You know what? Stop worrying about what others think. Think about what you think of yourself. When you take responsibility and express true **remorse**, you'll grow as an individual. Feeling sorry for what you have done is a good thing. You won't be the weak person you were in the middle of the night. You'll be a strong person who can **recognize** your mistakes.

B **UNDERSTANDING MEANING FROM CONTEXT** **Match the words from the reading (1–4) with their meaning (a–d). Then underline the words in the text that helped you guess the meaning.**

1 forgiveness _____   a the feeling that you are sorry for something bad you have done

2 flaw _____   b admit that something that is often unpleasant is true

3 remorse _____   c something about us that shows we are not perfect

4 recognize _____   d no longer being angry at someone who has done something bad to you

2 LISTENING

A 🔊 **5.01** **Listen to the conversation. Check (✓) the things the man and the woman mention.**

1 The man says what he did wrong. ☐

2 The woman gives advice about making apologies. ☐

3 The woman tells Marco words he should not use in an apology. ☐

4 The man says what happened after he apologized. ☐

3 **WRITING**

A   Read the note of apology. Underline the parts where the writer uses the same language in two different sentences. Then replace the repeated words with words from the box.

offer you this gift   ~~his behavior~~   his service

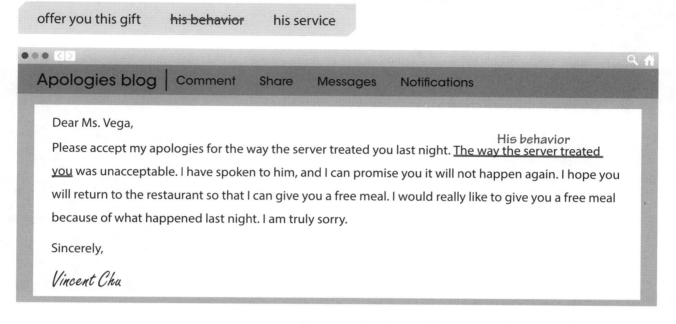

Apologies blog | Comment   Share   Messages   Notifications

Dear Ms. Vega,

Please accept my apologies for the way the server treated you last night. <u>The way the server treated</u> <u>you</u> was unacceptable. I have spoken to him, and I can promise you it will not happen again. I hope you will return to the restaurant so that I can give you a free meal. I would really like to give you a free meal because of what happened last night. I am truly sorry.

His behavior

Sincerely,

Vincent Chu

B   You are the owner of a clothing store. Last week, a sales clerk in your store was rude to a customer. Write an apology to the customer. Use the email in exercise 3A as an example.

_____

_____

_____

CHECK AND REVIEW

Read the statements. Can you do these things?

UNIT 5	Mark the boxes. ☑ I can do it. ? I am not sure. I can …		If you are not sure, go back to these pages in the Student's Book.
VOCABULARY	☐	use specific terms to describe different types of stories.	page 44
	☐	use expressions to talk about making and breaking plans.	page 46
GRAMMAR	☐	order events in the past using the past perfect.	page 45
	☐	use *was/were going to* and *was/were supposed to* for plans in the past that changed or were cancelled.	page 47
FUNCTIONAL LANGUAGE	☐	react to problems and disappointing news.	page 48
	☐	accept bad news.	page 49
SKILLS	☐	write an apology.	page 51
	☐	avoid repetition in writing.	page 51

UNIT 6 COMMUNITY ACTION

6.1 HELPING OUT

1 VOCABULARY: Describing communities

A **Complete the conversations with the words in the box.**

bring together	connect with	donate
get involved with	get to know	help out
join	pass on	take care of
~~take part in~~	volunteer	

1 A There's a community garden meeting next week. Would you want to go with me?

   B Yes, I'd like to ___take part in___ that.

2 A Would you like to become a member of our organization?

   B Yes, I'd really like to _____ .

3 A I was wondering if you'd like to give some money to our organization.

   B Sure, I'd be happy to _____ .

4 A Who watches your children when you're at work?

   B My parents _____ them.

5 A Do you have a lot of friends in your new neighborhood?

   B Not really. I need to _____ more people.

6 A I don't get paid for the time I work at the hospital. I do it for free.

   B It's very nice of you to _____ .

7 A My classmates and I have a lot in common.

   B It's good that you have people you can _____ .

8 A Let me carry those boxes for you.

   B It's very kind of you to _____ . Thank you.

9 A Let's have a street party so that all the neighbors can do things with each other.

   B Yes, it will be good to _____ everyone in the neighborhood.

10 A These are the websites that will answer everyone's questions.

   B OK, thanks. I'll _____ the information.

11 A Why did you start to volunteer at the after-school center?

   B I wanted to _____ a group that helps children.

B **Complete the sentences so that they are true for you.**

1 I connect with people by ___talking about sports___ .

2 I've never donated to _____ , but I'd like to.

3 It would be fun to join _____ .

4 I want to get involved with _____ soon.

5 A good way to bring neighbors together is by _____ .

6 It's important to take care of _____ .

2 GRAMMAR: Present and past passives

A Underline the object of the sentence. Then rewrite the sentence using the present or past passive tense.

1 Someone donated <u>millions of dollars</u>.
   Millions of dollars were donated.

2 People know the organization all over the world.
   _____

3 Someone started the shelter 50 years ago.
   _____

4 People give free clothes away every day.
   _____

5 Somebody serves the food three times a day.
   _____

6 People left their pets on the streets.
   _____

B Complete the sentences with passive verb forms. Use the verbs in parentheses ( ).

1 I _____*am given*_____ (give) different things to do every week. That's why I like to volunteer.
2 We _____ (help) right away. It didn't take long for someone to see us.
3 The boys _____ (send) to a different room because they had arrived too late.
4 The students _____ (test) every Monday. They never like it.
5 A doctor _____ (call) when there is an emergency.
6 Our dog _____ (hit) by a car. We were so upset.

C Write yes/no and information questions. Use the passive. Then look online for the answers.

1 where / the United Nations / found *Where was the United Nations founded?*
   It was founded in San Francisco in the United States.

2 when / the UN building in New York / complete
   _____

3 the UN building in New York / design / by a Brazilian architect
   _____

4 visitors to the UN building in New York / require / to get a
   security pass _____

5 tours of the UN / give / in English only
   _____

1 VOCABULARY: Describing good deeds

A Circle the correct words.

1 People should be (grateful) / ungrateful for the kind / (kindness) of others.

2 You can show your appreciate / appreciation by saying "thank you."

3 I'm sorry Tom was so grateful / ungrateful after all the helpful / unhelpful things you did for him.

4 The only reward / rewarding I want is your success. That will be very reward / rewarding.

5 Sometimes I get advice that is really helpful / unhelpful. People say things to me without thinking.

6 I appreciate / appreciative everything you have done for me.

7 We were very appreciate / appreciative of their act / action of kindness.

8 It was very appreciative / thoughtful of our neighbors to send food after the fire. I hope we showed our grateful / gratitude.

9 When you help someone with something, you are lending a helping hand / showing your appreciation.

10 It was a thoughtful gesture to offer to help repair / think about repairing the broken window.

B Answer the questions. Use your own ideas.

1 How do you show your appreciation for acts of kindness?

_____

2 Who do you like to lend a helping hand to?

_____

3 Why are thoughtful gestures important?

_____

4 What kinds of things are you grateful for?

_____

5 Do you think helping others is its own reward?

_____

6 How do you react if someone is ungrateful for help you offer?

_____

2 GRAMMAR: Passives with modals

A Match 1–6 in column A with a–f in column B.

A

1 Animals here at the zoo should not _____c_____
2 Your homework must _____
3 Donations to the charity can _____
4 New homes might _____
5 Thank you so much for everything. Your kindness will _____
6 Young children should _____

B

a be remembered.
b be taught to be polite.
c be given any kind of food.
d be found for the homeless.
e be finished by tonight.
f be sent at any time.

B Complete the sentences using passives with modals. Use the words in parentheses ( ).

1 Before you help people, they _____should be asked_____ (should / ask) if they want help.
2 I promise that the report _____ (will / finish) before I leave.
3 This _____ (can't / do) by one person. You need help.
4 Tori _____ (might / give) a job at the animal shelter.
5 I think more money _____ (should / spend) on animals.
6 The boy's injury is serious. He _____ (must / take) to a hospital right away.

C Answer the questions using passives with modals and the words in parentheses ( ). Then write another answer to the question using passives with modals and your own ideas.

1 What can happen at home? (food / cook in a microwave oven)

Food can be cooked in a microwave oven.

Clothes can be washed in a washing machine.

2 What must happen at airports? (bags / check)

_____

_____

3 What should happen in parks? (children / watch)

_____

_____

4 What will happen in your next class? (we / give a homework assignment)

_____

_____

5 What might happen in stores? (customers / tell the wrong price)

_____

_____

6.3 THERE'S NO NEED ...

1 FUNCTIONAL LANGUAGE: Making offers

A **Complete the conversations. Use the words in the box. Write two more conversations using your own ideas.**

anyway	appreciate	can	good
kind	let	like	manage

1 **A** Would you _____ to sit down?

   B I'm OK. Thanks _____.

2 **A** _____ I help you with those grocery bags?

   B Thanks, I really _____ it.

3 **A** _____ me get the door for you.

   B I can _____.

4 **A** Do you need a hand with that?

   B That's very _____ of you.

5 **A** I'm getting up. Do you want my seat?

   B Nope, it's all _____.

6 **A** _____

   B _____

7 **A** _____

   B _____

2 REAL-WORLD STRATEGY: Imposing on somebody

A **What do the people request? Put the words in the correct order. Write a response either accepting or refusing the request. Then think of two more requests and responses.**

1 I'm / but / sorry / is it / if / OK

   Ana _____ I use your phone for a moment?
   Mine is out of battery.

   _____.

2 I / don't / but / mind / rude / would you / to be / mean

   Joe _____ letting me go ahead of you in
   line? I only have a few items, and I'm in a rush.

   _____.

3 _____.

4 _____.

   _____.

46

FUNCTIONAL LANGUAGE AND REAL-WORLD STRATEGY

A   Offer to help the person in the picture. Then write the person's response.

1

A _____

B _____

2

A _____

B _____

3

A _____

B _____

4

A _____

B _____

B   Read the situations. Write a request and a response. Use *I'm really sorry to have to ask …* or *I don't mean to be rude …* to make the requests.

1   Bernardo and Marta are co-workers. Their boss is waiting for their report by 5 p.m. but Bernardo gets a call that his son is sick. Bernardo has to leave. Marta doesn't have to leave.

A _____

B _____

2   Your car has broken down and won't be repaired for a few days. You need a car for a job interview tomorrow. Your neighbor has two cars.

A _____

B _____

PAINTING SAFER STREETS

1 LISTENING

A 🔊 **6.01** **LISTEN FOR GIST** **Listen to the conversation about guerilla gardening. Check (✓) the topics that Angela mentions.**

What guerilla gardening is	☐
Why she started guerilla gardening	☐
The places she has done guerilla gardening	☐
Other countries where guerilla gardening happens	☐
Some of the problems with guerilla gardening	☐

B 🔊 **6.01** **LISTEN FOR DETAIL** **Listen again. Write *T* (true) or *F* (false).**

1 Greg and Angela both do guerrilla gardening. — F

2 People do guerrilla gardening to improve public spaces. — ___

3 City governments help with guerrilla gardening projects. — ___

4 People can send donations if they want to support guerrilla gardening. — ___

5 Guerrilla gardening groups exist only in North America. — ___

6 Businesses are helping guerilla gardening groups. — ___

2 READING

A **Read about guerrilla gardening in Los Angeles, California. Circle the correct answers.**

Guerrilla gardening started back in the 1970s and has grown into an international movement. In some places, people do it to make public spaces more beautiful; in other places, they do it to grow food. In South Central Los Angeles, it was very difficult in the past to find healthy food. That's why a movement was started to grow vegetable gardens on city property. An organization, L.A. Green Grounds, was formed and started planting fruit trees and vegetables. The gardeners were all volunteers and came from all over the city and many different professions. Green Grounds has helped to change a community. There is plenty more space that could be improved. The city of Los Angeles owns nearly 26 square miles of empty land. That's enough land to plant 725 million tomato plants!

1 Guerrilla gardening started *a few /* (*many*) years ago

2 In the past, people had to drive far to buy *fast food / healthy food*.

3 L.A. Green Grounds was started in order to *make the community beautiful / grow food*.

4 Volunteers for L.A. Green Grounds *all live / do not all live* in South Central Los Angeles.

5 The city of Los Angeles *owns / does not own* a lot of empty land.

A Read the report. Find the quotations and circle the phrases that are used to introduce them. Then underline the verbs that are used in the phrases.

The city has a lot of empty space that could be used for guerrilla gardening. A recent report by Our Community Together has made a list of the possible places. One of the leaders of the group claimed that "many parts of the city are ugly because nobody takes care of them. Using those spaces to grow plants will make the city more beautiful."

When asked for comment, one resident said, "I think this is an excellent idea. We could start with the Greenwood section of town. Right now it is full of trash. It should be cleaned up."

However, not everybody agrees. One person in city government pointed out that "the city has a lot of needs. The empty space could be used for day-care centers and libraries."

It is true that cities have many needs, but we must accept that having beautiful spaces is one of those needs.

B Think of an empty space in your town that guerrilla gardening could improve. Write a report about the space. Write about where it is, how big it is, what the space looks like right now, and how it could be changed. Include at least one quotation. You can make up the quotation.

_____

_____

_____

_____

_____

_____

CHECK AND REVIEW

Read the statements. Can you do these things?

UNIT 6	Mark the boxes. ☑ I can do it. ? I am not sure. I can …	If you are not sure, go back to these pages in the Student's Book.
VOCABULARY	☐ use verbs and verb phrases to describe good works.	page 54
	☐ use expressions and different forms of words to talk about good deeds.	page 56
GRAMMAR	☐ use the passive voice in the simple present and simple past.	page 55
	☐ use the passive voice with the modals *can*, *might*, *must*, and *will*.	page 57
FUNCTIONAL LANGUAGE	☐ make, accept, and refuse offers.	page 58
	☐ politely impose on someone.	page 59
SKILLS	☐ write a report about a community project.	page 60
	☐ introduce quotes.	page 60

1.5 TIME TO SPEAK Job interviews

A **Which of the following do you think are common interview questions in your country? Write two more interview questions. Why do you think companies ask these questions?**

Where do you see yourself in five years? ☐

Are you married? ☐

What is your greatest weakness? ☐

How much did you make in your last job? ☐

B **How would you answer the questions you checked in exercise A? Write your answers.**

2.5 TIME TO SPEAK Restaurant rescue

A **Think of a restaurant you don't like in your town. Make a list of the things you don't like about it.**

B **Write a letter to the owner offering suggestions on how he/she can improve the restaurant.**

3.5 TIME TO SPEAK A whole new lifestyle

A **Read the beginning of the story below. Complete the story with an expected change in Erika's lifestyle. Go online and find three pictures to help tell the story.**

In college, Erika wanted to travel the world. But a year after Erika just graduated college, she was still living with her parents. She hadn't found a job yet, and she certainly didn't have money to travel. This was *not* how she had planned her life. So she decided to …

B **Share the photos in the next class. Can anyone guess your story?**

4.5 TIME TO SPEAK Design an ad

A **Look online for an ad written in English. Write a description of the ad.**

- What product is it selling?
- Where does the ad appear? On television? On a website? On a billboard?
- What advertising techniques does it use?
- Do you think the ad is effective? Why or why not?

B **Describe the ad in your next class. Are your classmates familiar with the ad? Do they agree with your opinion of the ad?**

5.5 TIME TO SPEAK A chance meeting

A **Look back at the story on page 52 of the Student's Book. Then answer the questions.**
  - What happens in the story?
  - What kind of story is it?

B **Choose one of the story types below. Change the details of the story on page 52 of the Student's Book to fit the new story type.**
  - coming-of-age story
  - mystery
  - success story
  - tear jerker

C **Present your new story at the next class. Can your classmates guess the new story type?**

6.5 TIME TO SPEAK Your urban art project

A **Go online and find an urban art project somewhere in the world that you think is interesting.**
  - What is the project?
  - Where is it?
  - Who is involved in the project?
  - What are the goals of the project?

B **Write a report about the project and bring it to the next class. Explain it and discuss it with the rest of the class.**

NOTES

The authors and publishers acknowledge the following sources of copyright material and are grateful for the permissions granted. While every effort has been made, it has not always been possible to identify the sources of all the material used, or to trace all copyright holders. If any omissions are brought to our notice, we will be happy to include the appropriate acknowledgments on reprinting and in the next update to the digital edition, as applicable.

Photographs
Key: B = Below, BL = Below Left, BR = Below Right, C = Centre, CL = Centre Left, CR = Centre Right, TC = Top Centre, TL = Top Left, TR = Top Right.

All the photographs are sourced from Getty Images.

p. 2 , p. 53: Hero Images; p. 3: Boris Breuer/The Image Bank; p. 4: maroke/iStock/Getty Images Plus; p. 5: shironosov/iStock/Getty Images Plus; p. 7, p. 55: Jose Luis Pelaez Inc/Blend Images; p. 10: Tony C French/The Image Bank; p. 11: foxestacado/iStock/Getty Images Plus; p. 12: Eisenhut and Mayer Wien/Photolibrary; p. 13: Alain Schroeder/ONOKY; p. 14: XiXinXing; p. 15: altrendo images/Altrendo; p. 16: petekarici/E+; p. 18: JGI/Blend Images; p. 19: SKA/Cultura Exclusive; p. 20: dardespot/E+; p. 21: Jon Feingersh/Blend Images; p. 22 (TR): Kwangmoozaa/iStock/Getty Images Plus; p. 22 (BL): Asia Images Group; p. 23: Yagi-Studio/E+; p. 24: vinhdav/iStock Editorial/Getty Images Plus; p. 26: AfricaImages/iStock/Getty Images Plus; p. 27: Stewart Bremner/Moment; p. 29: Benjamin Torode/Moment; p. 30: Yellow Dog Productions/The Image Bank; p. 31: SolisImages/iStock/Getty Images Plus; p. 32 (TR): PhotoAlto/Milena Boniek/Brand X Pictures; p. 32 (CR): Mauro-Matacchione/iStock/Getty Images Plus; p. 34: kzenon/iStock/Getty Images Plus; p. 35: LWA/The Image Bank; p. 37: AntonioGuillem/iStock/Getty Images Plus; p. 38: martin-dm/E+; p. 39: BakiBG/iStock/Getty Images Plus; p. 40: tommaso79/iStock/Getty Images Plus; p. 42: Blend Images - KidStock/Brand X Pictures; p. 43, p. 51: Tetra Images; p. 44: fstop123/iStock/Getty Images Plus; p. 45: Mauro-Matacchione/iStock/Getty Images Plus; p. 46: Maskot; p. 47 (TL): ElenaNichizhenova/iStock/Getty Images Plus; p. 47 (CL): Mikael Vaisanen/Corbis; p. 47 (TR): HASLOO/iStock/Getty Images Plus; p. 47 (CR): Jupiterimages/Photolibrary; p. 48: Johner Images.

Front cover photography by Alija/E+.

Audio production by CityVox, New York.

Corpus
Development of this publication has made use of the Cambridge English Corpus (CEC). The CEC is a multi-billion word collection of contemporary spoken and written English. It includes British English, American English, and other varieties. It also includes the Cambridge Learner Corpus, the world's biggest collection of learner writing, developed in collaboration with Cambridge Assessment. Cambridge University Press uses the CEC to provide evidence about language use that helps to produce better language teaching materials. Our Evolve authors study the Corpus to see how English is really used, and to identify typical learner mistakes. This information informs the authors' selection of vocabulary, grammar items and Student's Book Corpus features such as the Accuracy Check, Register Check, and Insider English.